This Nature Storybook belongs to:

_____

_____

_____

_____

WALKER BOOKS

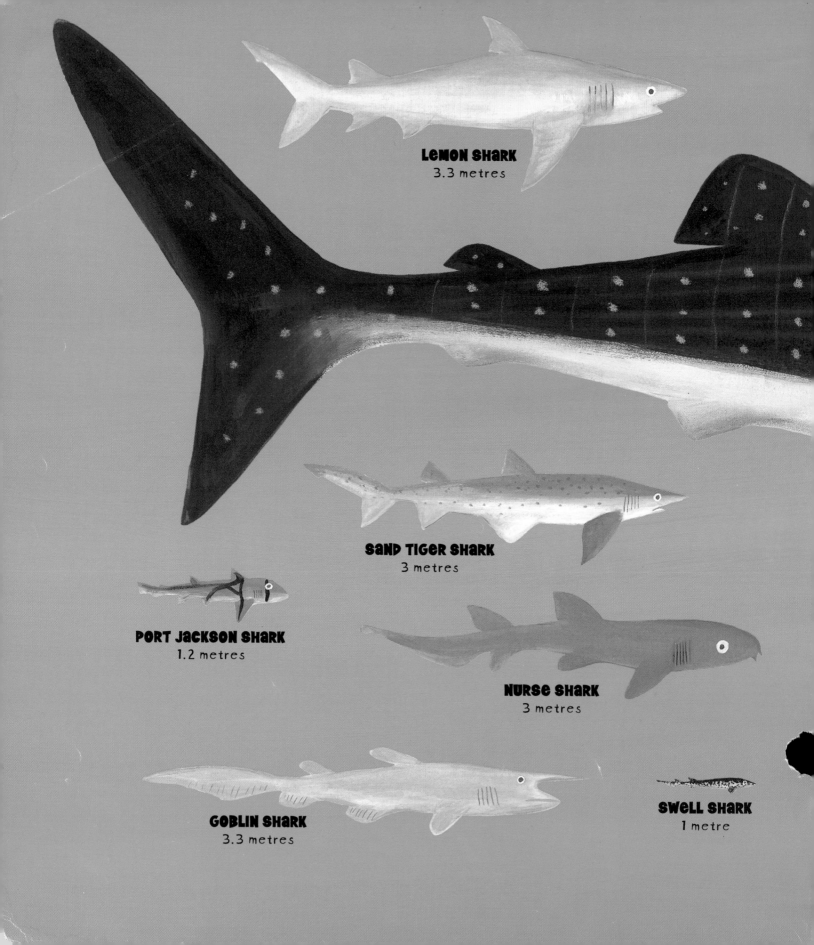

LEMON SHARK
3.3 metres

SAND TIGER SHARK
3 metres

PORT JACKSON SHARK
1.2 metres

NURSE SHARK
3 metres

GOBLIN SHARK
3.3 metres

SWELL SHARK
1 metre

DWARF LANTERN SHARK
0.17 metres

BULL SHARK
3.2 metres

WHALE SHARK
12 metres

COOKIE-CUTTER SHARK
0.4 metres

ZEBRA SHARK
2.5 metres

TIGER SHARK
5 metres

For the children of Hudson Primary
School, Sunderland. N.D.
For Mum, Dad, Lisa
and Wayne
J.C.

First published 2003 by
Walker Books Ltd
87 Vauxhall Walk
London SE11 5HJ

This edition published 2015

1 2 3 4 5 6 7 8 9 10

Text © 2003 Nicola Davies
Illustrations © 2003 James Croft

This book has been typeset in Blockhead and Sitcom

Printed in China

British Library Cataloguing in Publication Data:
a catalogue record for this book is
available from the British Library

ISBN 978-1-4063-6697-6

www.walker.co.uk

SURPRISING SHARKS

Nicola Davies

illustrated by
James Croft

WALKER BOOKS
AND SUBSIDIARIES
LONDON • BOSTON • SYDNEY

Wait for me!

You're swimming in the warm blue sea.
What's the one word that turns your
dream into a nightmare?
What's the one word that
makes you think of
a **giant**
man-eating
killer?

Shark? Yes, it is a shark!

It's a **DWARF LANTERN SHARK**.
The smallest kind of shark in the world, it is
just bigger than a chocolate bar. Not a giant,
certainly no man-eater and only a killer
if you happen to be a shrimp.

You see, **MOST** sharks are not at all what you might expect. After all, who would expect a shark to ...

Like all **LANTERN SHARKS** this **BLACKBELLY LANTERN SHARK** can make light shine from its tummy. This helps it to blend in with the silvery surface of the sea and avoid ending up as dinner for bigger fish.

have built-in fairy lights ...

or blow up like a party balloon ...

SWELL SHARKS swallow water when they get scared and blow up to three times their normal size so that they can wedge themselves between rocks and no predator can pull them out.

This Australian shark is called a **WOBBEGONG**. Its patterned skin matches the rocks and corals on the sea floor, so it can sneak up on shellfish, crabs and small fish unseen.

lie on the sea floor like a scrap of old carpet...

HAMMERHEAD SHARKS have eyes and nostrils on the ends of their "hammers". It helps them to pin-point the scent of prey and gives them all round vision.

...or look like tools from a monster's DIY kit?

SAW SHARKS root out fish hidden in sand and mud with their "swords", then grab them with their needle-sharp teeth.

In fact, sharks come in all sorts of shapes and sizes.

BLUE SHARK

COOKIE-CUTTER SHARK

NURSE SHARK

ANGEL SHARK

GOBLIN SHARK

How can such different animals all be sharks?
Look carefully and you'll see
all the things they share.

DORSAL FIN

TAIL

PELVIC
FIN

FINS AND TAIL FOR SWIMMING...
A shark's tail fins are bigger at the top
than at the bottom, unlike other fish's
tails. Their tails push them through the
water and the fins help them to swim
left or right, up or down.

PECTORAL
FIN

Outside:

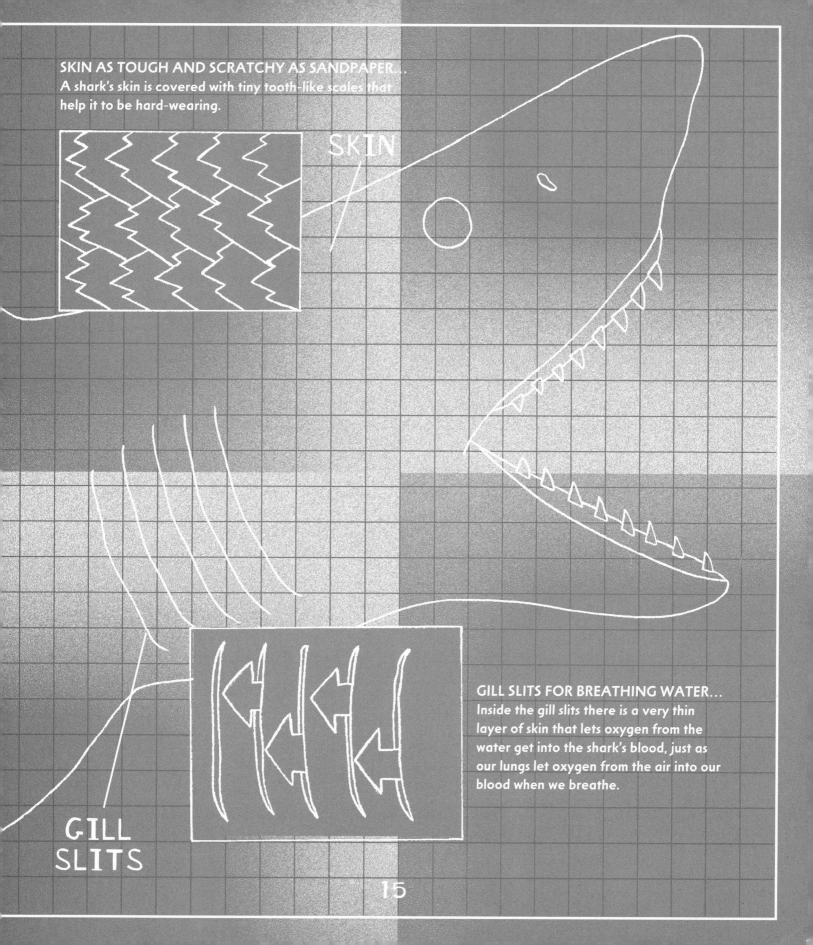

SKIN AS TOUGH AND SCRATCHY AS SANDPAPER...
A shark's skin is covered with tiny tooth-like scales that help it to be hard-wearing.

SKIN

GILL SLITS FOR BREATHING WATER...
Inside the gill slits there is a very thin layer of skin that lets oxygen from the water get into the shark's blood, just as our lungs let oxygen from the air into our blood when we breathe.

GILL SLITS

15

Inside:

Sharks' jaws aren't part of their heads like ours are. Instead they're held on by a kind of living rubber band, so the jaws can shoot forward fast to grab prey.

JAWS

TEETH

ROWS AND ROWS OF SPARE TEETH, SO THAT THE SHARK IS NEVER WITHOUT ITS BITE
A shark can have up to 3,000 teeth, all in rows one behind the other. As one tooth wears out, the one behind moves forward to replace it. So sharks always have sharp teeth and use more than 20,000 in their lifetime.

A BENDY, BONELESS SKELETON THAT HELPS STOP IT SINKING…

Sharks' skeletons are made of a tough kind of the stuff called cartilage – the same thing that your ears and the end of your nose are made of. Cartilage floats in water like a rubber ball.

SKELETON

But it isn't the basic body plan that makes sharks sharks …

it's the **sharkish** way they behave!
Sharks are always hungry and they're
always on the lookout for their next meal.
Some even start **killing**
before they're born.

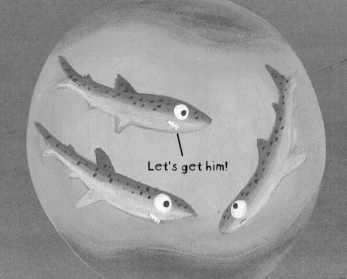

SanD TIGER SHarKS
give birth to just two
live young — which is all
that's left after those two
have eaten the other six
babies in their mother's belly.

Let's get him!

Some sharks lay eggs and some give birth to live
young. But all baby sharks are just like their
parents, with **sharp teeth** and
the ability to hunt right from the start.

18

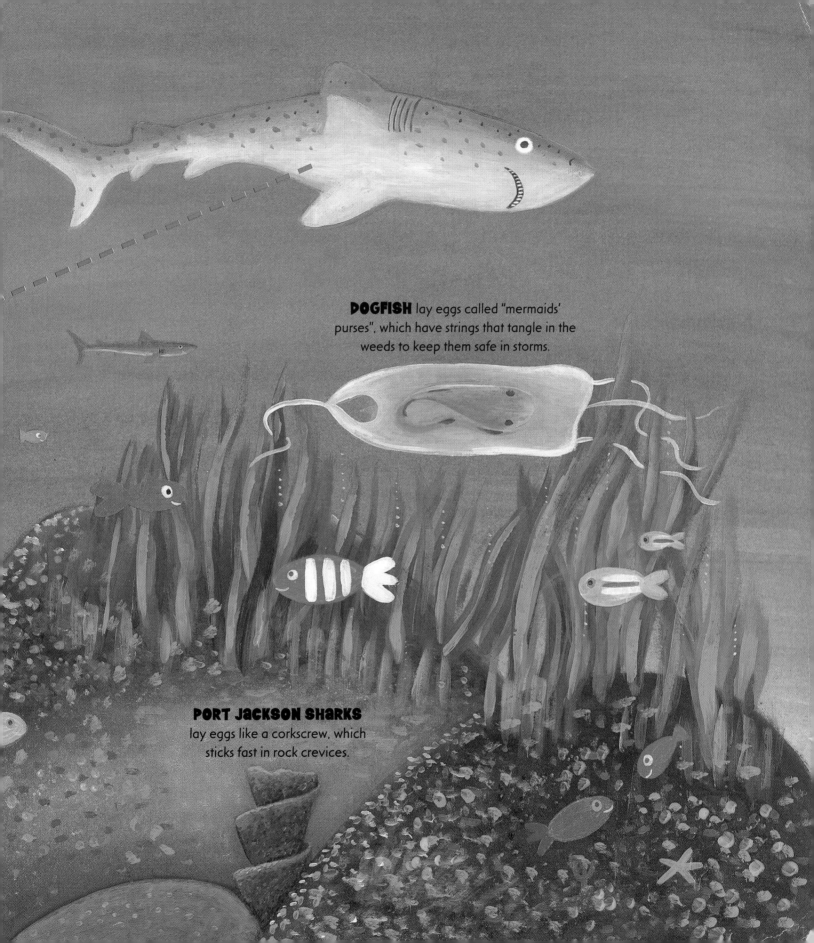

DOGFISH lay eggs called "mermaids' purses", which have strings that tangle in the weeds to keep them safe in storms.

PORT JACKSON SHARKS lay eggs like a corkscrew, which sticks fast in rock crevices.

Sharks' senses are fine-tuned, ready for the tiniest hint that might mean food!

Sharks have tiny holes to let sound into their inner ears. They can hear sounds that are too low for our ears to pick up.

Sharks' eyes are on the sides of their heads, so they can see almost as well behind them as they can in front!

The whole of a shark's skin is sensitive in the same way that your fingertips are. You can tell hot from cold, rough from smooth, moving from still. A shark can also get all sorts of information from the movement and temperature of the water all around its body.

To a hungry shark, the faintest trail of clues is as clear as a restaurant sign.

A shark's nostrils are just under the tip of the snout. Water flows into them as the shark moves forward, bringing any scents with it.

Gel-filled pits in a shark's nose can detect food. Every animal has nerves, which are like cables carrying electrical messages around the body. The shark's gel pits can sense this electricity.

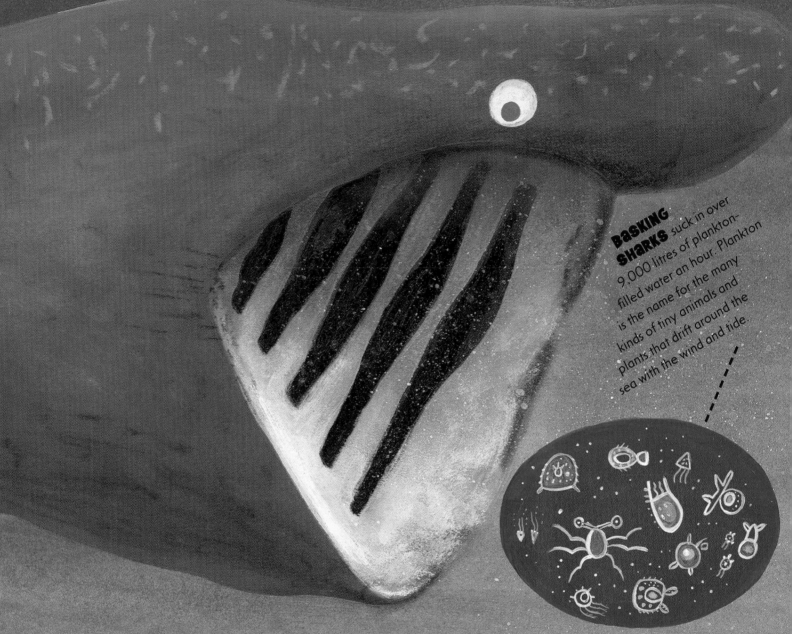

BASKING SHARKS suck in over 9,000 litres of plankton-filled water an hour. Plankton is the name for the many kinds of tiny animals and plants that drift around the sea with the wind and tide.

And when at last they're close enough for the kill, they feel the **crackle** of their prey's living nerves, so they bite in just the right place ... no matter what the prey! Whether it's **plankton** ...

or **people**! Oh yes, it's true – some sharks do kill people; about six of us every year.

The **GREAT WHITE** is one of just three species of shark that attack people regularly. The other two are the **BULL SHARK** and the **TIGER SHARK**. In fact, only 30 of the 500 different kinds of shark have ever attacked humans. Crocodiles, elephants, dogs and even pigs kill more people every year than sharks do!

But every year **people** kill **100 million** sharks.

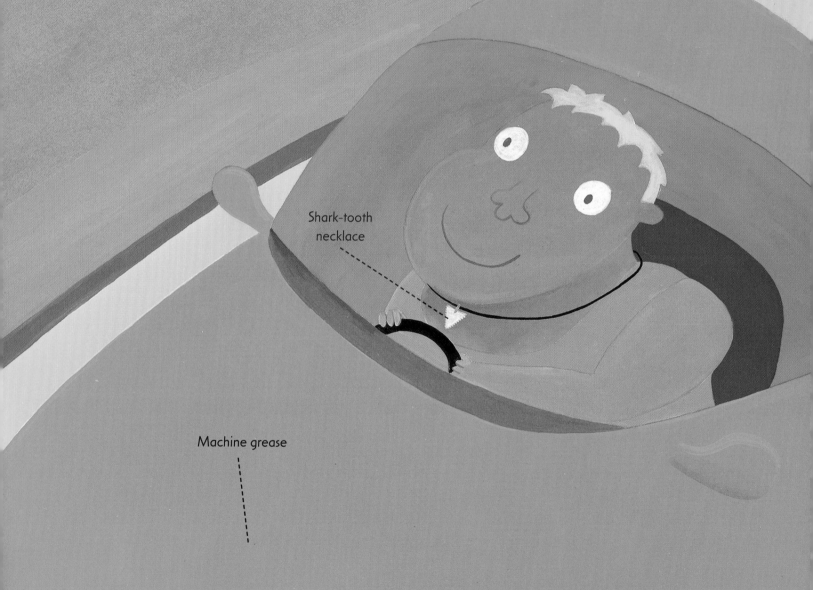

Shark-tooth necklace

Machine grease

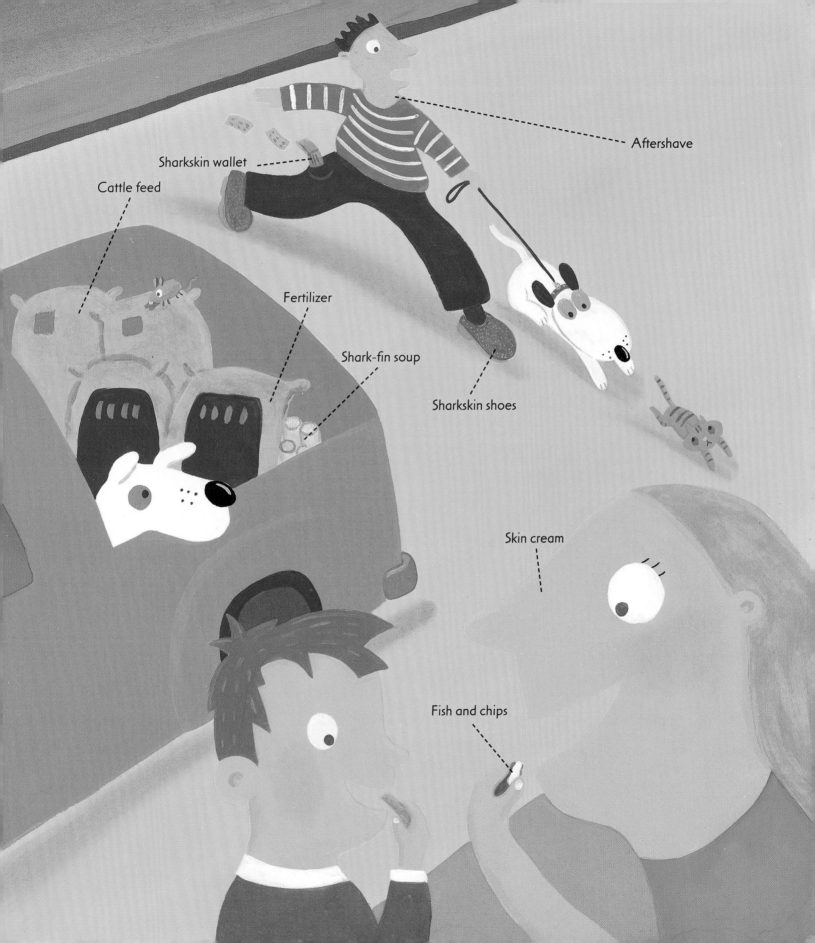

Aftershave

Sharkskin wallet

Cattle feed

Fertilizer

Shark-fin soup

Sharkskin shoes

Skin cream

Fish and chips

If you were a shark swimming in the lovely blue sea, the last word you'd want to hear would be . . .

hUMaN!

Index

Look up the pages to find out
about all these shark things.
Don't forget to look at both
kinds of words – this kind
and this kind.

About Sharks

Sharks have been on earth for 300 million years and can be found today in every ocean and sea in the world. People see sharks as monsters, but of the 500 different kinds of shark in the world, only thirty have ever attacked humans and most feed on shellfish and small fishes.

Sharks are predators, they kill only to eat and are as important in the sea as wolves, lions, tigers and bears are on land.

About the Author

Nicola Davies is a zoologist and writer with a special love of the sea. She has seen basking sharks off the Devon coast and once came face to face with a shark whilst snorkelling – a baby spotted dogfish that was the size of a sardine. As sharks have been on earth a lot longer than humans, she feels they deserve our respect and protection.

About the Illustrator

James Croft has always enjoyed drawing sharks. Their teeth, speed and danger have always fuelled his imagination like no other creature.

James lives and works in London.

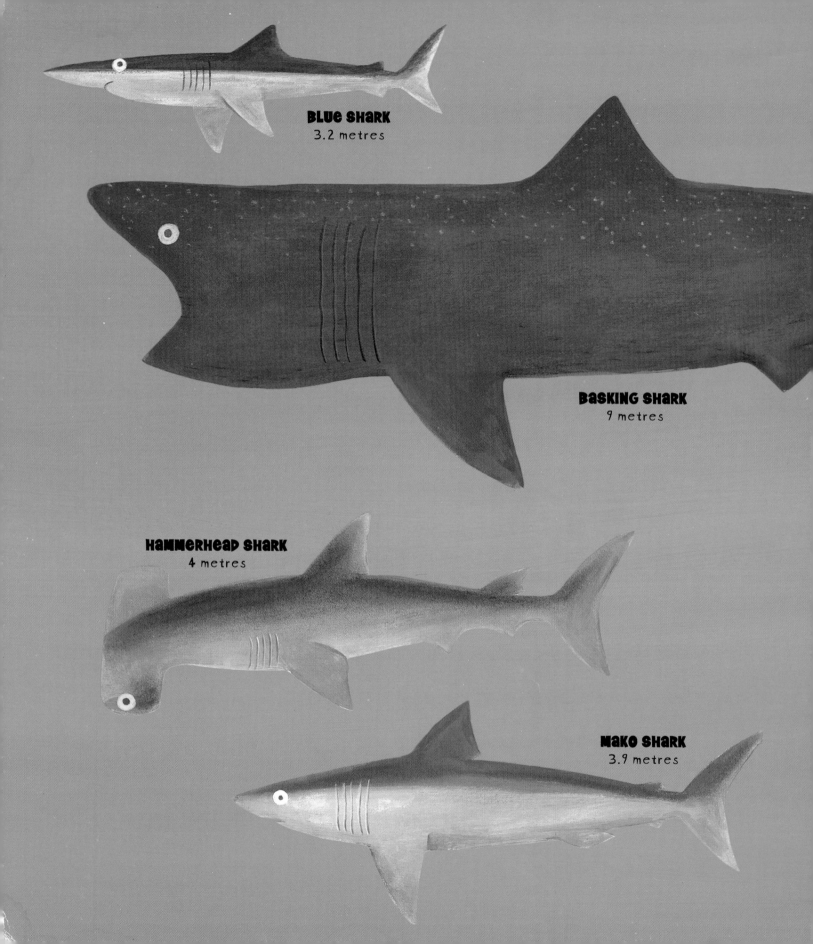

BLUE SHARK
3.2 metres

BASKING SHARK
9 metres

HAMMERHEAD SHARK
4 metres

MAKO SHARK
3.9 metres

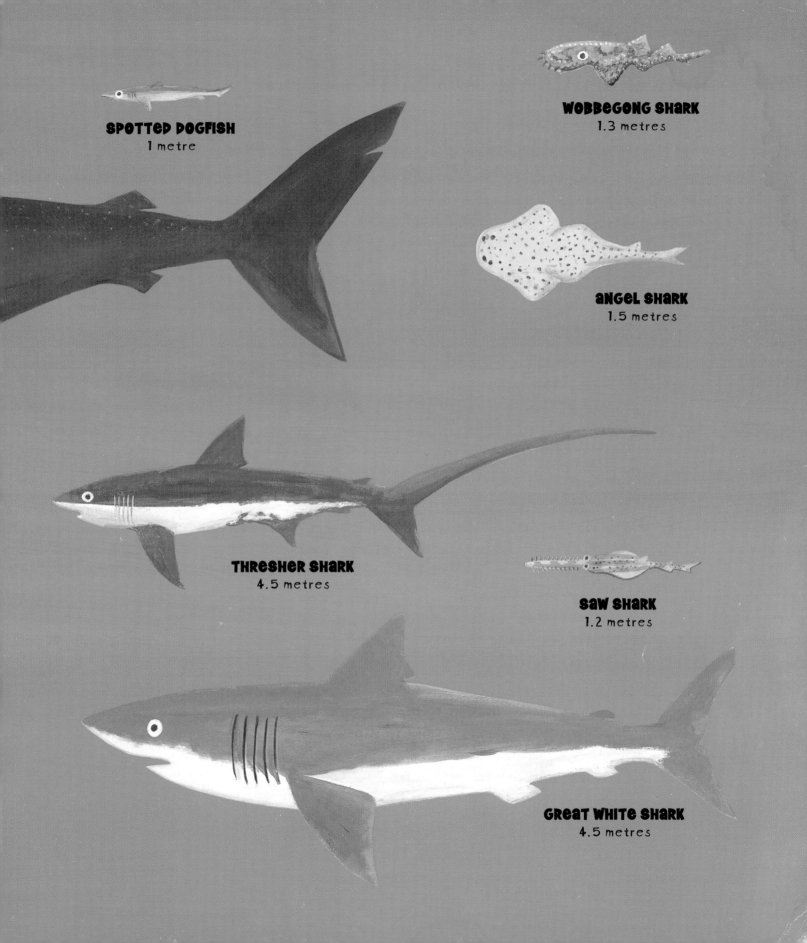

SPOTTED DOGFISH
1 metre

WOBBEGONG SHARK
1.3 metres

ANGEL SHARK
1.5 metres

THRESHER SHARK
4.5 metres

SAW SHARK
1.2 metres

GREAT WHITE SHARK
4.5 metres

Note to Parents

Sharing books with children is one of the best ways to help them learn. And it's one of the best ways they learn to read, too.

Nature Storybooks are beautifully illustrated, award-winning information picture books whose focus on animals has a strong appeal for children. They can be read as stories, revisited and enjoyed again and again, inviting children to become excited about a subject, to think and discover, and to want to find out more.

Each book is an adventure into the real world that broadens children's experience and develops their curiosity and understanding – and that's the best kind of learning there is.

Note to Teachers

Nature Storybooks provide memorable reading experiences for children in Key Stages 1 and 2 (Years 1–4), and also offer many learning opportunities for exploring a topic through words and pictures.

By working with the stories, either individually or together, children can respond to the animal world through a variety of activities, including drawing and painting, role play, talking and writing.

The books provide a rich starting-point for further research and for developing children's knowledge of information genres.

Nature Storybooks support the literacy curriculum in a variety of ways, providing:

- a focus for a whole class topic
- high-quality texts for guided reading
- a resource for the class read-aloud programme
- information texts for the class and school library for developing children's individual reading interests

Find more information on how to use Nature Storybooks in the classroom at
www.walker.co.uk/naturestorybooks

Nature Storybooks support KS 1–2 English and KS 1–2 Science